Suppose your town is about to choose a new mayor. How will you do it?

You'll vote!

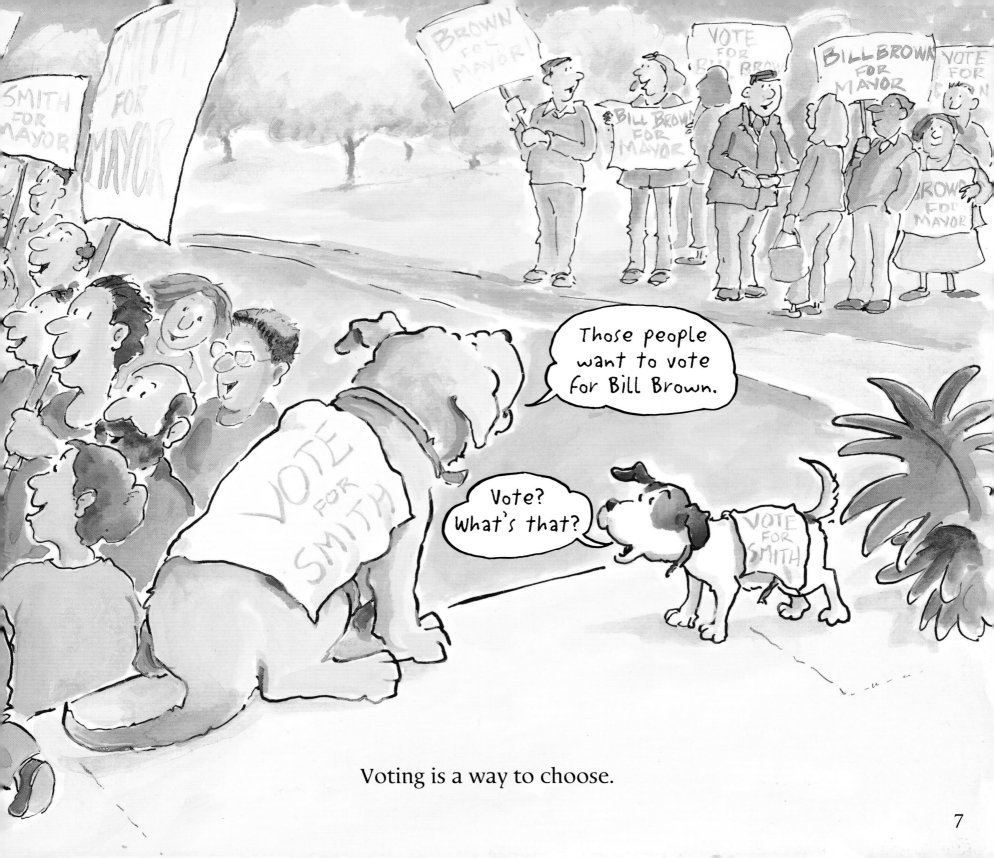

Voting is a way to choose.

You can vote for favorite books, movie stars, candy bars . . .
or even puppies!

If someone wants to be elected mayor, she needs to convince as many people as possible to vote for her!

Many people just don't vote. Why not?

Maybe they think their vote is like a little drop of water in an enormous ocean. Their vote *is* only one out of many, many votes. But sometimes the winner of an election is decided by just a few votes.

Who decided who could vote?

When this country began, the Founding Fathers wrote a constitution. It said how we would govern ourselves. It said people should vote; but it didn't say *who* could vote. That was left to each state to decide. And that was a problem!

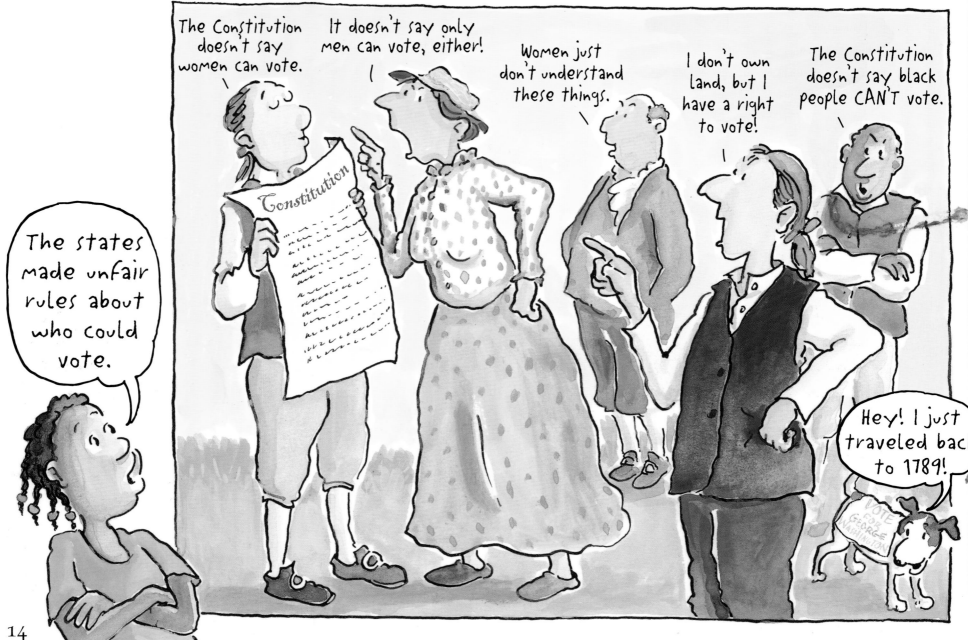

Angry people protested. They wrote letters. They held rallies and made speeches. They marched, were arrested, and went on hunger strikes. Some were killed trying to claim their right to vote. But it took many years, four amendments to the Constitution, and several new laws before all citizens, 18 years or older, were allowed to vote.

If you want to vote, you need to register. Where? At your town office. Or you can download a registration form from the Internet, or you might even find a booth set up at a shopping mall or at a political rally.

Do you want to join a political party? You've probably heard of the Democrats and the Republicans. But you could join the Green Party, the Libertarians, the America First Party, or the Progressives, to name just a few. Or you could be independent and not join any party at all.

Before you vote, you'll need to find out about the different candidates. How? Read newspapers, watch TV news, listen to the radio, or surf the Internet. Do you agree with their ideas?

You might have a chance to hear the candidates debate.

You might even be able to ask questions!

Before an election, everyone tries to guess who will win. Pollsters ask some of the voters whom they're planning to vote for. Then they estimate who will be the winner. But voters can change their minds.

How can you help your candidate win? You can volunteer to answer phones, call voters, address envelopes, or hand out flyers. Campaigns need lots of help.

And they need lots of money to help pay for phones, computers, stamps, flyers and bumper stickers, and, most of all, ads and more ads! Where will they find the money?

You might want to donate a few dollars to your favorite candidate's campaign. Or maybe you'll be invited to a fundraising dinner. Would you like to pay $250 for a fancy hamburger and a chance to meet the candidate?

If you donate lots of money, maybe the candidate will listen to you more than to other voters. Is that fair? Does that mean your vote will count more than other voters' votes? There's a lot of disagreement about this.

By the last week of the campaign, everyone is tired. But the candidates make more speeches. They shake more hands, and they run more and more ads. Maybe, just maybe, they will convince another few voters to vote for them!

Some of these ads can be very misleading.

Finally, it's Election Day.

Most voters are assigned a particular place to vote—a school, a library, a church basement—wherever there is space for voting booths. What if you're away on voting day? You can get an absentee ballot in advance. Some places let people vote by mail or on the Internet. A few places set up voting machines early. But however you vote, you get just one vote. You can't go back and vote again!

In most places, people use voting machines. Many cities and towns are replacing old machines with new electronic ones. But in very small towns, voters still mark paper ballots with a pencil. However you do it, you'll vote in a private booth. No one can see how you vote.

When the voting ends, the counting begins! Who will win? Stay close to your TV, radio, or the Internet to find out.

Usually a few hours after the polls close, the winner is announced.

BUT WAIT!

What if the election is won by only a few votes? The candidate who lost can ask that the votes be counted again. Then it could take a few days—or longer—to carefully recount the ballots and find out who really won.

At last, the election is decided. In the end someone does win . . .
and someone does lose.

You aren't happy? You wish the other candidate had won?
Well, remember, the mayor works for everyone—even the people
who didn't vote for her. She'll need to listen to *all* the voters.

After she is sworn in, the new mayor will have a few years to do her new job.

She won't please all the people all the time, but if she does a good job, maybe the voters will elect her again!

41

DO YOU KNOW THESE WORDS?

Absentee ballot—A mail-in ballot used by people who will be away on voting day.

Ballot—A sheet of paper or a card that is marked by the voter when he or she votes.

Campaign—A series of events and activities designed to help a candidate get elected.

Candidate—The person who's trying to get elected.

Debate—An organized public discussion between the candidates about the issues.

Democracy—A type of government in which people choose, by voting, whom they want as their leaders and how they want their country governed.

Election—The casting of votes to decide who will hold a political office.

Gerrymandering—When voting districts are redrawn in a way that favors one political party over another. This means some voters in the opposing party are left without an equal voice.

Independent—A person who does not join a political party.

Issues—Problems that are debated or discussed by the candidates.

Party—A group of people who join together because they share similar ideas about how the country should be governed.

Poll—A survey of people's opinions.

Polling place (or the polls)—Where voters go to vote.

Pollster (or polltaker)—A person who finds out what people are thinking.

Recount—Counting the ballots a second time because of a very close election.

Voter ID laws—Laws that require voters to show identification to vote in national, state, and local elections. These can be non-photo ID laws, which allow voters to use documents like a bill or paycheck to verify their identity, or photo ID laws, which require identification with a photo—such as a driver's license or passport.

Voter suppression—Anything that makes it harder for eligible voters to be able to vote and have their votes counted. This includes fewer polling places, fewer days when people can vote, voter ID laws, and gerrymandering.

Voting district—Cities, counties, and states are divided into voting districts. Voters can only vote in their assigned district.

43

TIMELINE OF VOTING RIGHTS

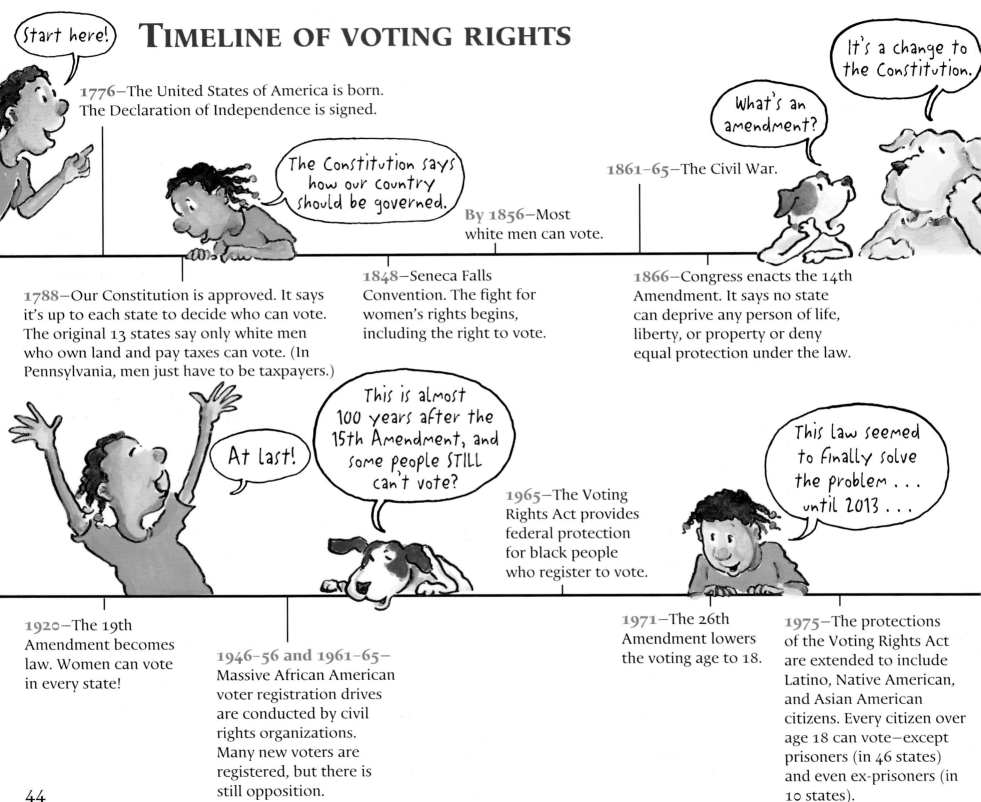

Start here!

1776–The United States of America is born. The Declaration of Independence is signed.

The Constitution says how our country should be governed.

By 1856–Most white men can vote.

What's an amendment?

It's a change to the Constitution.

1861–65–The Civil War.

1788–Our Constitution is approved. It says it's up to each state to decide who can vote. The original 13 states say only white men who own land and pay taxes can vote. (In Pennsylvania, men just have to be taxpayers.)

1848–Seneca Falls Convention. The fight for women's rights begins, including the right to vote.

1866–Congress enacts the 14th Amendment. It says no state can deprive any person of life, liberty, or property or deny equal protection under the law.

At last!

This is almost 100 years after the 15th Amendment, and some people STILL can't vote?

1965–The Voting Rights Act provides federal protection for black people who register to vote.

This law seemed to finally solve the problem . . . until 2013 . . .

1920–The 19th Amendment becomes law. Women can vote in every state!

1946–56 and 1961–65– Massive African American voter registration drives are conducted by civil rights organizations. Many new voters are registered, but there is still opposition.

1971–The 26th Amendment lowers the voting age to 18.

1975–The protections of the Voting Rights Act are extended to include Latino, Native American, and Asian American citizens. Every citizen over age 18 can vote—except prisoners (in 46 states) and even ex-prisoners (in 10 states).

The 14th Amendment didn't help much.

So another amendment was written.

But some states had "poll taxes" and difficult tests that kept black people from voting.

The first woman is elected to Congress, but most women still can't vote?

1870—The 15th Amendment says that the vote shall not be denied on account of race or color.

867—The first black oter registration drive held.

1868—In the South, the Ku Klux Klan disrupts voting with a campaign of terror, lynching and beating some black people who tried to vote.

By 1913—Ten states allow women to vote: Wyoming, Colorado, Idaho, Utah, Washington, California, Arizona, Kansas, Oregon, Illinois.

1917—Jeannette Rankin is the first woman elected to the U.S. Congress. She is from Montana, where women can vote.

1917—Over 200 women are arrested for civil disobedience while calling for women's voting rights in a national campaign. Many are imprisoned.

1788—1975! That's 186 years before everyone was able to vote.

What's in the future?

2002—The Help America Vote Act provides states with money to buy new voting machines and makes sure no voter is turned away and every vote is counted.

993—The National Voter Registration Act makes it asier to register to vote.

2000—There's a big problem counting votes in the presidential election and a big disagreement over who won! What's the solution?

2013—Part of the Voting Rights Act is struck down by the U.S. Supreme Court, allowing states with a history of discriminating against marginalized voters to change voting laws without federal approval.

2016—For the first time in U.S. history, more than 200 million people are registered to vote, marking a major milestone in voter registration efforts.

MORE ABOUT POLITICAL PARTIES

What are the two main political parties in the United States today?
The Democratic Party and the Republican Party.

What are their symbols?
The Democrats have a donkey. The Republicans have an elephant.

Are there other political parties?
Yes! The Green, Libertarian, Socialist, Independence, America First, and Reform parties have all promoted candidates in recent elections. In the past there were the Know-Nothing, Free-Soil, Bull Moose, and Whig parties—to name a few.

Do candidates have to belong to a political party?
Political parties try to help their candidates win, but there are candidates who prefer to be independent of any party.

What happens when there are candidates from more than two parties in an election?
There's a chance that none of the candidates will win more than fifty percent of the vote. If that happens, often there is another election (a runoff) between the top two vote getters. But many people think that a better solution would be for voters to rank the candidates in order of preference, indicating their first choice, their second choice, and so on. Then the candidate with the fewest votes would be eliminated and the votes counted again. What about the voters who picked the losing candidate as their first choice? Their second-choice votes would be counted. This process would be repeated until one candidate ended up with a majority of the votes—the winner! This idea is called "instant runoff."

Which parties have won presidential elections?
Between 1778 and 2016, there have been 19 Democratic, 19 Republican, 4 Whig, 2 Federalist, and 1 National Union presidents.

The Dogwaggers believe in soft couches, juicy bones, and Sparky for Mayor Dog.

I'm starting the Dogwaggers Party.

The Dogwaggers' symbol will be our cat, Bubbles.

RESOURCES

Would you like to know more about voting? Here are some resources that were available when I wrote this book. For further updates, refer to my website at christelow.com and click on "Classroom Connections."

archives.gov (the National Archives)

fairvote.org

kidsvotingusa.org

loc.gov/learn/features/election (scroll down and select Elections from the list of presentations)

lwv.org (the League of Women Voters)

pbskids.org/democracy/vote

rockthevote.com

votesmart.org

Many thanks to Karen Carlson and her fourth-graders
and to Michael Krasner, for their helpful comments

Copyright © 2003 by Eileen Christelow
All rights reserved. Originally published in hardcover in the United States by Clarion Books,
an imprint of Houghton Mifflin Harcourt Publishing Company, 2003.

For information about permission to reproduce selections from this book,
write to trade.permissions@hmhco.com or to Permissions,
Houghton Mifflin Harcourt Publishing Company, 3 Park Avenue, 19th Floor, New York, New York 10016.

hmhco.com

The illustrations were executed in pen and ink and acrylic gouache.
The main text was set in 17-point Magellan. The balloon text was set in Litterbox.

The Library of Congress has cataloged the hardcover edition as follows:
Christelow, Eileen.
Vote! / Eileen Christelow.
p. cm.
Summary: Using a campaign for mayor as an example, shows the steps involved in an election,
from the candidate's speeches and rallies, to the voting booth where every vote counts,
to the announcement of the winner.
1. Voting—United States—Juvenile literature. 2. Elections—United States—Juvenile literature.
3. Political campaigns—United States—Juvenile literature. [1. Voting. 2. Elections.
3. Politics, Practical.] I. Title.
JK1978 .C48 2003

ISBN: 978-0-618-24754-7 hardcover
ISBN: 978-0-618-48606-9 paperback (2004)
ISBN: 978-0-547-05973-0 paperback reissue (2008, 2012)
ISBN: 978-1-328-49922-6 paperback reissue (2018)
ISBN: 978-0-547-85915-6 ebook

Manufactured in China
SCP 10 9 8 7 6 5 4 3 2 1
4500713757